100
PROGRESSIVE STUDIES
without Octaves.

Revised and fingered by
Max Vogrich.

C. CZERNY, Op. 139. Vol. I.

8.

Allegretto con moto.

9.

Allegro.

4

Allegro.

12.

Andantino.

16.

22.

23.

24.

25.

12

Allegro, quasi presto.

29.

Marcia. Allegro maestoso.

30.

31.

Allegretto vivace.

32.*)

Allegro moderato.

*) The pupil should be able to play the scales fluently in all the keys, if he is to derive full benefit from the following more difficult pieces.

15

36.

40.

46.

Moderato à la Marcia.

52.

58.

59.

Andantino con dolcezza.

60.

Allegro.

61.

100
PROGRESSIVE STUDIES
without Octaves.

Revised and fingered by *Max Vogrich.*

C. CZERNY, Op. 139. Vol. II.

68.

Allegro moderato.

p sempre legato.

39

✤) Ped. (Pedal) means that the foot should press down the damper Pedal, until directed by the proper sign (✳)
to release it.

The pupil must play the following scales, without the notes, daily; and must recite to his teacher the number of sharps (♯) or flats (♭) in each, at every lesson.

48

50

54

84.

Allegretto vivace.

85.

Andantino.

86. Allegro marcia.

legato sempre.

Allegro con moto ed espressivo.

87.

Allegro molto.

88.

89.

Allegretto.

Andantino.

Andante à la marcia.

92.

Andante grazioso ed espressivo.

93.

97.

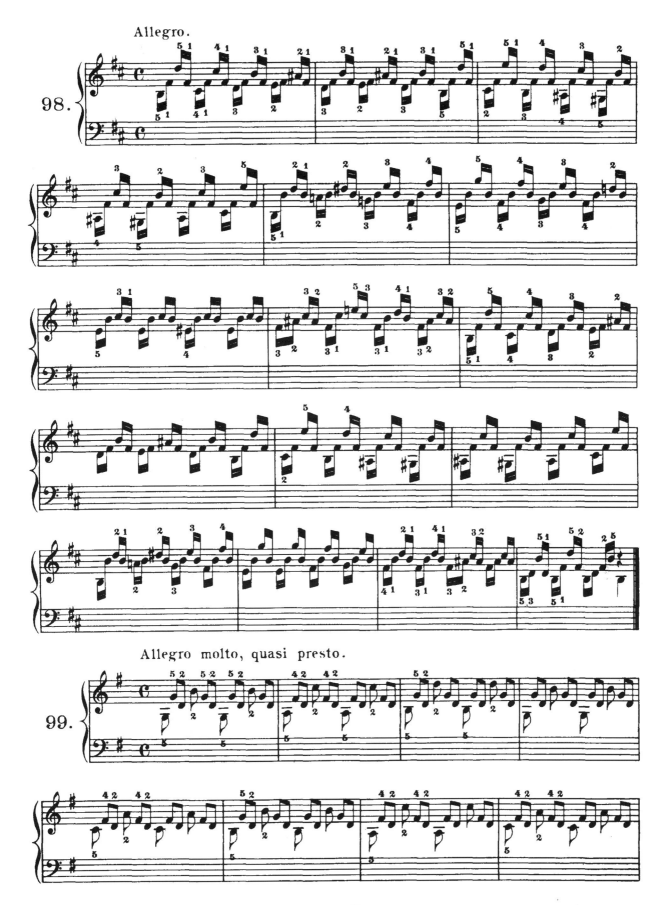

Presto.

100.

p leggieriss.

Manufactured by Amazon.ca
Bolton, ON

28091251R00042